I0078929

These Unblessed Days

These Unblessed Days

Poems by

Greg Huteson

© 2022 Greg Huteson. All rights reserved.
This material may not be reproduced in any form, published,
reprinted, recorded, performed, broadcast,
rewritten or redistributed without
the explicit permission of Greg Huteson.
All such actions are strictly prohibited by law.

Cover design by Shay Culligan
Cover image by Benjamin Huteson

ISBN: 978-1-63980-152-7

Kelsay Books
502 South 1040 East, A-119
American Fork, Utah 84003
Kelsaybooks.com

To Jill Peláez Baumgaertner and Paul Mariani

"No . . . friendship can ever cross the path of our destiny without leaving some mark upon it forever."
Francois Mauriac, *The Desert of Love,* trans. Gerard Hopkins

Acknowledgments

The author gratefully acknowledges the following publications in which many of the poems first appeared.

Alabama Literary Review: "Homestead," The Store Room," "Enter into Life"

Better Than Starbucks: "A Morning Word"

BigCityLit: "The Necessity of Lancing"

Blue Unicorn: "A Matter of Preference"

The Brazen Head: "The Break of Day"

Convivium: "Apocalypse"

The Crank: "The Caregiver"

FORMA: "The Ferry Ride"

Grand Little Things: "Last Hour"

The Honest Ulsterman: "Eating Dragon Fruit," "Sunday Rest"

Innisfree Poetry Journal: "Little Egrets"

MacQueen's Quinterly: "To Dream of Hospitality"

Modern Age: "Marred Desires"

A New Ulster: "Watches of the Night"

The Road Not Taken: "These Unblessed Days"

Saint Katherine Review: "Descended into Hell," "Gaps"

THINK: "Tropical Market"

Trinity House Review: "An Honest Man's Words"

Contents

Marred Desires

If less of mud than minerals and marl,
still it's true mankind was formed by God
of uncursed soil and neatly contoured rib.
The disparate elements a gracious sign
of Deity not yet obscured by dusk.
And there was evening, as the Good Book says.

But then there was the stark and brooding dawn.
We are there yet in that unsubtle place,
toe-teetered on the line between the light
and viscous dark, although some still believe
we're in the third day with its muddied earth
and spotted fruit with its ambiguous seeds.

Averse to leave the saturated dirt
or set aside the slush of lust and pride,
we daub our cheeks and nails with particles
of pliant clay to augment and impress,
our speckled features thicker and more coarse
than when first shaped and fired by nimble God.

Then, sweating in the piercing sun we weigh
our large and unassuaged desires and thirsts.
At last to quench them, climb the outlawed tree
to take and eat the surely pleasing fruit.
Much later, breathless from this exercise,
we'll scrape our skin with broken shards, ashamed.

Watches of the Night

Grimly flog the dark and its slate cloud
and, sore and sweaty, crease the feathered pillow.
Then, panting, swing the hip with pain and loud

sore croak and settle deftly on the right,
the swayback mattress' side that's near the wall.
A barrier to blank the street's orbed light.

Sigh, then mumble brief and begging prayers.
Mutter lists of courteous words for God
while interjecting "please" and "darn unfair."

The spoor of rams soon litter half the mind.
A sure reminder you can't count on sheep
to quiet or be stilled despite a line

of darting, nipping prayers. Then thin-mouthed, stare
at wall, at ceiling, set on waiting out
the black, the lack of mercy. Cupboards bare.

To Dream of Hospitality

Once more will the tiles so welcome friends
or witty guests across the threshold board
for tea and talk and watermelon seeds?

And will the green door in the whitewashed hall
as aptly crack and open as an egg
that's tapped against a peeling countertop?

The bamboo stools at ebb, will they be set
around the coffee table and the chairs
of polished cypress, delicate but kind?

And what, friend, of the sorghum liquor flask?
Will you nip it from the cabinet shelf
and tuck it somewhere handily nearby?

For then you'll squat there nattering away
the night with cups of oolong tea and shots
of Kinmen liquor under the autumn moon.

The Break of Day

Though still, I'm ringed by flocks of middling angels,
smudged guardians of no specific rank.
They are half-bored and overlook
my seafood porridge and my tilted chair,
even the cautious pigeon on the ledge.

Now with these spirits, there's no need to quake
or craven urge to fall and then revere.
They are too simple, motley, and too dull.
And while they stand and watch, these lax recruits,
they sometimes shuffle in their stained white boots.

Once breakfast's done, ceramic bowl aside,
I tug my leather Bible from the shelf
and knock the *Songs of Innocence* askew.
The wooly beings start to twist and squirm
despite the faces, wings, and dervish wheels.

They yawn at these symbols in Ezekiel one.
The languor of familiarity
is my conjecture of the likely cause.
Impiety? Who knows, for they are not
inclined to speak, these dingy, fretful ones.

The Lamb and golden throne are more their choice
than a pine desk and scruffy leather book
illuminated by an alley light.
The yellowed rag quilt, it discomfits them
as do the tiles and drifting strands of dust.

I fear that they aspire to a raise,
a quick promotion to a senior rank,
a place, say, in a holy man's small guard.
That or the ranks around a seraph chief,
a speedy end to skirting my divan.

The Bible closed, I stand and lift my hands
to pick the firstfruits of the autumn day,
then shuffle to the door. The angels wait
in twos and threes to file out and grunt,
halfheartedly, of lethargy and doom.

A Morning Word

Beitun District, Taichung, Taiwan

A word the dark-splotched dog seems not to know,
the bougainvillea rousted on the walls,
the pose of scooters all on edge to crow.

The rice with deep-fried dough at roadside stalls,
the drowsy child with bag half dragged to school,
the tai chi bodies swayed in rhyme like dolls.

The angled park with posted list of rules,
the watercourse with intermittent fish,
the small brick shrine with incense sticks as tools.

The egg crepe fresh laid on a plastic dish,
the turnip cake with dab of savory sauce,
the cup of soy milk silky as a fish.

The scarred, damp pilings with their marks of moss,
the hissing of the air brakes on a truck,
the smog that hints the bridge's chance of loss.

The siren parting someone from their luck,
the dove jongleurs chorusing their coos,
the myna hopping from the rocks to muck.

The wail on hearing of the neighbor's news,
the cat on wall as silent as a stone,
a word for hours as mournful as the blues.

The Caregiver

Long addled by a thread of cultic thoughts,
the pensive woman tended ritual bones—
the pelvic bone, femurs, backbone, and skull—
that she had draped within the wheelchair's frame
at six that steaming morning for this stroll.

Her steady hand propped up the scaffolding
much like an aide that's avid for the stage.
Soon, as she pushed across the frond-lined park,
the pigeons flitted in erratic rows
to flee her rattling load for quiet grass.

Along a concrete wall among her friends
a few steps' distance from a jungle gym
and with their fleshless, slack-limbed charges near,
she listened to a convoluted tale
of porridges and pills and less and less to eat.

The liturgy of this, the call/response
of it, the lapping murmurs of the rest,
might mark the place as sacred ground, she thought,
and cracked her knuckles absentmindedly
while peering at the oak tree leaves for nymphs.

The words all said, the morning petered out,
she stood and stretched and raised her holy hands.
In just a moment, she would grab the grips
glued on the relic's battered leather chair
and walk, now cleansed, back to the red wood door.

These Unblessed Days

They say the sun itself is clay.
They say the moon is marble.
But I am far too panicked now
to stare at mineral displays
or ponder soil marvels.

They say that peace will come just then,
the pacifists will surely reign.
But signs in heaven, blood on earth
are teachings I was raised on.
There is no clever juggler queen

or prince to toss the world to rights
and set the props then harmless down.
The water is a crystal ring,
the birds a loop of bamboo kites
that bob and jig around.

But I'm too fear-struck for the gaze,
too weighted for these unblessed days.

Descended into Hell

On the slate gray plain,
paused when jabbed by rain
bloodying as darts,
I rub pricked parts
hard with salty hands,
mull intention and
providence that sent
me from shabby rent
propped along the sea.

Raw abrasions mat,
drenched with gray-brown splats.
Blur like fingerpaint.
But there is no plank,
lean-to, shack or slight
overhang in sight.
No odor of wild greens,
cornbread, pork or beans
on the luckless wind.

On the shortgrass plain
wandering in pain,
vision bound and snot
turgid through the clots
of neckerchief and beard—
sweat and salt and tears.
Skull well-bruised and numb,
near delirium
I choke and praise the Lord.

Creeds self-mumbled low—
sotto voce low—
hardly cross near-washes,
rivulets and grasses.
Sprinkle ferrets lightly,
warn coyotes but slightly.
How profligate the awe and fear!

An Honest Man's Words

It is as if each one were scheme
or plot, the line of an attack,
initial pressure of the steam

that thrusts an engine over track.
As if each were the word of God,
the alpha of a sovereign knack

that would, if clever, sever sod
from house or man from wife or rows
from gardener, splinter good from God.

It is as if each one were blows
that shatter drums and raw-most hearts,
abrupt imperatives of crows

that caw and fill the air with darts
at lesser birds that flee to brakes
that will, they hope, have quiet parts.

Were imprecations, bilious snakes
with rattles and unnerving eyes
that give each grayish rodent shakes.

As if each phrase were hazard's guise,
another wallop on the beam
that links us all in small white lies.

Gaps

Most of a most scrawny rectangle of sky
leans across the gap, planking the edge
of one white building to another.
The concrete paths and stoops
horn shoulder-wide between the walls.
The alley floor—all cockeyed runnels
and rickety slabs—is here and there
slick with water (faucet, dishes, clothes)
and on one short jag with moist crap
shovel-splattered from the sewer.

A man with jeans hitched on narrow hips
slouches on a scooter, head bent in cocksure
reverence to his iPhone or its Samsung imitation.
His fingers skitter on the screen
while he mumbles to the girl
beside the basin on the ramp, notched
entrance to a store stocked with bottles
of brown and yellow drinks, cigarettes
and Hello Kitty face masks. Her hands are quick
at wringing soggy leggings. Her head lifts.

A Matter of Preference

Xuanguang Pier, Sun Moon Lake, Taiwan

As if three hundred steps
were there to tempt our day.
They weren't. And need I say,
they failed to halt our steps
to Ah Po's tea leaf eggs.

The marbled charcoal air,
a horse's mis-set head—
a golden figurehead—
had led us to this pier
and tourist portico.

The map of Sun Moon Lake,
the tour boat workers' words
aligned with lessons heard
some decades since that, take
the famous places here,

it's this that is the win.
The white and briskly red-
lined mark of keen, well-bred
respect for someone's kin.
Pagoda on the ridge.

But disinclined to climb
and teased by earthy smells,
we peeled our steaming shells
and ate the brown egg whites
with their shiitake hints.

A Kitchen Tale

He was a rather pious pot,
a rotund saint of fragrant broth,
although he slept on burlap cot
and wore a hat of checkered cloth.

She was a fractious frying pan,
a sturdy frame for bacon grease.
She popped and sizzled at her man
then cooled at night to rigid peace.

The children were five knives and spoons,
a dullish lot but deft as swords.
They clanked when washed and swore like loons
when laid out on the drying boards.

Their house a room, three beds, a door,
a cookbook and a food scraps bin.
A wobbly pump just out the door
to rinse their stubborn stains and sin.

One day she fell and with a clang
she landed on a crooked board,
in exile from her usual hang
but scarcely noticed by her "lord."

The spoons and knives spied from the shelf,
a drooping incline on bent slides.
They mocked their maw and cussed himself
and whacked each other's tarnished sides.

Apocalypse

If by the steps the old man, Flip,
a gnarled wisp with whiskered face,
his smoke tucked in arthritic grip,
and if he leans beneath a card
that lists a hefty smoking fine
and glares out at a latent yard,

And if he mumbles like a bear
then lifts his jaundiced eyes to God
or not to God but smoggy air
and starts to smoke and snubs the murk
while kids and fathers saunter by
and mothers race in cars to work…

The courtyard's quiet for the nonce
though vivid orchids drop their scraps
and long-tailed pigeons scout out haunts
to bide the humid heat, for dreams
and ecstasies of fallen fruit
that somehow lodge in hidden seams.

Then by the steps the wisp that's Flip
at long last thumps the butt with grace,
the tumbling scrap a smoky blip.
It settles on a square of yard,
soon starts an active, crackling blaze
that puts the neighbors on their guard.

They grouse then, shortly, shout their fears
and fling their blackened words at God
or not at God but cunning bears,
the burly ones who fight the flame
while dogs and kittens frolic on
and leopards lope in pairs, untame.

The Necessity of Lancing

Lance the boil on your calf.
If it's necessary, pinch it
as you grit your teeth and gasp
while staring at the shuddering wall.

Have a cotton kerchief handy
to absorb the pus and swab
the cinctured wound, the wet
that courses down your luckless leg.

Have the kerchief ready also
for other lumps and waters, on jaunts
and travels and long, stiff nights
beside certain beds and at all wakes.

On occasion, carry the lancet with you,
but not to church or funeral homes.
An ice pick will do, with a plastic lighter
to sterilize the steel. The intention:

Not to wound or threaten harm
or nick God's enduring furcate image,
but to relieve taut skin or unclog jams
in thin brass pipes in a stranger's home.

Hobble to the bathroom or the sink
in the kitchen island. Poke or jab
and poke or jab again and, as you lance
the boil on your calf, let the waters flow.

Eating Dragon Fruit

All through, it's a profligate color.
Magenta with small, black seeds.
And all the while its bright skin
is too ruddy much. Each thallus
a reminder of a greeny world
of fields marked and marred
with clambering, fragile stems.

The fruit, slightly chilled, is sui generis,
a distinct commodity, a blessing
in firmness and coolness. The stain
of its flesh is a caution and delight
for famished children and aesthetes
attentive to small puddles of juice
neat as archipelagoes on the marble table.

The trick is not to lift each dripping cube
with a toothpick. No, set the toothpick aside
for the smallest of metal forks.
The flesh of the fruit is far too soft
for a single tine. On that path lies disaster.
The wrong tool may lose this snack.
The last, glorious piece no longer yours.

Sunday Rest

Where has the early autumn sun
just tucked itself and gone and hid?
All's grackle-smooth and goat-back bare.
No loose hung squibs, unraveled light.

The chastetree skips and jigs above
the divots of the patio.
Its thin, bleached leaves mere kite tail rags
set bumbling in unmannered air.

Now will the drab dun carpet flare?
Or will it lie quiescent, bored
beside the egg-dull plastic blinds,
and wait the light rain's weightless end?

The drizzle drains to O and naught.
Inside, the carpet mulls a shrug
and shake before another nap.
The crack-lined blinds turned down for shade.

Tropical Market

There are no proper doors
to this pavilion with its eggs and gourds
and crooked ducks, its stores
with stacks of swiftly sewn cloth shirts and shoes.

There is a woody dusk
well tucked beneath the splotched aluminum
and iron—frame and husk
and staging for the sellers' plywood stalls.

The path's between two boards
with loads of oranges, limes, and mountain teas.
Just beyond are hoards
of chicken meat and pork and heaps of beef.

While farther in, a space
is harshly bright. Fluorescent lights hang down
from rusty screws in place
since early days and far fans sway the chains.

Little Egrets

Alack! The little egret calls
(or warbles) as she loosely flaps
behind the curved neck of her mate.

And when with shrug of saint-white wings
he stalls in staggered air and cracks
the marsh-green water, lands and stands,

she glides and slips her yellow feet
into the thin canal quite near.
Her beak she dips for private fish.

Though separately they stalk and hunt,
their crests, white plumes, so lift and bob
as if the headdress on one head.

Not one but two, thin pitchers firm
within the water's structured tug,
no more unbalanced than the reeds.

They elegantly bend and pour
their efforts toward the narrow shade,
the underpinnings of the road.

With slips and care and backtracking
for bugs, an odyssey of mud,
they drain into that concrete dark.

Homestead

A culvert and a rusty metal shed,
a thorny clover patch, a metal grate,
a fence arthritic as an old bat's wing,
a red wood wagon and a willow sprig.
A bench swing on a shabby pinewood porch,
a nest for skunks beneath the buckled house,
concavities that sag with spiders' weight.
A grove of oaks, a hound dog, and a boar.
Or if not boar then armadillo pair.
Alert they are, with leather shells intact,
curves not yet cratered by a jacked-up truck.
A long dirt path that's cut with sand clay ruts.
A creek that smells of onions, stocked with bass.
A dearth of prints along its muddy bank.

The Store Room

1

It's dusk or seems so.
A lone white bulb is newly on,
revealing oddments and budget furniture.
Underneath, a white card table leans.
One end is draped with white
cleaning cloths. There's dust
on the spare, shadowed floor.

2

From right to left: a gray cabinet,
squat shelves, a pine desk,
a cork board. Pinned lightly on the cork,
there's a verse of Saint Paul's about heaven
and "Life is like a bowl of cherries."
A tad more left is a dark-framed window.
Outside, a washer, a mop, an expanse of sky.

3

Near the desk, on a soiled dun cloth,
are a kettle and a clay pitcher
with a few droplets on the rim.
There's a flimsy ironing board
near a bagged black-and-red fan.
And a chunky dehumidifier midfloor.
Streaks on one wall from a leaky AC.

A few steps in, the space is mainly shelves
and planks and cavities. Some for musty,
dusty thinkers' books, moldering facts,
analyses. And some for handier items.
Among them a spade, a tape measure,
a package from overseas. A canister
for tea, now empty. No last specks of green.

4

There's a desk lamp with a wood base
and a black shade. This is the lesser light.
For the ceiling bulb, there's a ladder.
The stashed umbrellas are dark, white,
and plaid while silver pots and crockpots
are unboxed and dull in a dozen crannies,
set widely among the miscellany.

5

There's even a slot for octopuses.
Plastic hangers, turquoise, red,
and black, with twenty-four arms among them.
A notch below them is a toolbox, its pale
latch dangling. Lower still, an insulated bag
for carbonated drinks, saltwater
fish, and other watery, wavery things.

On the far wall
is a cream-colored wardrobe
for ruined spreads and ruined quilts
in whites and sickly yellows. Even
the mothballs are dry, brittle, bland.
Even the roaches are scraps, mere straw.
The mirror's a half-flattened moon.

6

Not quite imaged by the mirror
is a scaffolding of "like new" suitcases, brown
and black with consort blues, but dusty.
A compact khaki sleeping bag on top.
There's a cairn of lumpy pillows,
precariously aslant. A spare door rests
in the corner, draped with a bright red cloth.

7

This store room, this sacristy,
is a tangle of devices
and sundry linens and lumber
and, yes, old plastic bags. Bags
within bags on the white tile
floor. The maranti door's half shut.
There's rest in these pistachio walls.

Last Hour

Beside the lime-green pillow and the spread,
he wriggled on a threadbare office chair
while typing lines with rhymes like "Fall" and "pall."

Outside was Texas' slumped and cheer-drained dusk,
mocked by a passing car's impertinence,
its vulgar engine wailing till it coughed.

The lonesome light bulb hardly held the desk
within its grimy halo. Or the door.
Or the walnut bureau and the glass.

While on the shade peonies dimmed and closed,
the spidered window caught the flitting light.
The words were sparse before his fingers stopped.

The Ferry Ride

As the captain rattles off his words,
the engine keens below his standard spiel,
a sorry groan beneath the lake's pale sun
that traces tourists to a solemn pier
of blackened timbers, shade, and granite slabs
on days of haze and curling dribs of fog.
Cracked tombstones lie beneath this misshaped lake
or so the quiet travelers are told
as separately they gaze and sigh and weep
sea tears that crowd their whitened, sandy cheeks
and swim their narrow bays of hands.
And when the captain says the nether shore is near,
the stubborn, ancient ferry rumbles on
to the dim-lit chill of its decay.

Enter into Life

A cup of water for the one in hell.
Go with the cup to quench his thirst.
It's better for you to enter Life
salted with fire and sacrificed with salt.

Go with the cup in your two hands.
And if a hand offends you, cut it off.
Salted with fire and sacrificed with salt,
you'll enter maimed into Life, your reward.

If your hand offends you, cut it off.
Likewise, cut off your crooked foot
and enter Life crippled, your reward.
It's better than being cast into hell.

Cut off your foot if it offends you.
It's better to be cast into the sea
with impediments than into hell,
where the fire will never be quenched.

It's better to be cast into the sea
than to offend one of the little ones
who believe the fire will not be quenched
and the worms and maggots will not die.

Pluck out your eye if it offends you.
A cup of water for the one in hell
is the gift of a one-eyed man.
It's better, by far, to enter into Life.

Salted, partial, and scorched,
but hobbling through freshets of joy.

About the Author

Greg Huteson is a missionary administrator. His poems have appeared in various US and UK quarterlies and literary journals, including the *Alabama Literary Review, The Honest Ulsterman, THINK, Modern Age, Innisfree Poetry Journal,* and *Trinity House Review.* He lives in Taiwan.

www.ingramcontent.com/pod-product-compliance
Lightning Source LLC
Chambersburg PA
CBHW030816090426
42737CB00010B/1293